GERMANY
Land of many Dreams

Featuring the Photography of Ric Pattison and Andrew Heaps
Text by Rupert O. Matthews.
CLB 1242
© 1987 Illustrations and text: Colour Library Books Ltd.,
    Guildford, Surrey, England.
Text filmsetting by Acesetters Ltd., Richmond, Surrey, England.
All rights reserved.
1987 edition published by Crescent Books, distributed by Crown Publishers, Inc.
Printed and bound in Barcelona, Spain by Cronion, S.A.
ISBN 0 517 46081 5
h g f e d c b a
Dep Leg. B-790-87

GERMANY
Land of many Dreams

Text by
Rupert O. Matthews

Foreword by
JOHN CARTER

CRESCENT BOOKS
NEW YORK

I'll admit right off that it took me a long time to get around to visiting Germany, though I must say in my defence that it wasn't entirely my fault. There always seemed to be very good reasons for going elsewhere, and the pressure to take other working trips was high. So Germany remained neglected until about four years ago, when I went to Bavaria and encountered the wild genius of King Ludwig the Second. I encountered it specifically in Neuschwanstein, the fairytale castle standing high and proud among the trees above Alpsee, and was thoroughly fascinated by the history of its construction. A theatrical designer did some sketches, apparently, and Ludwig simply took it from there.

It matched the mood of those times, with the legends of Tannhauser and Lohengrin inspiring its designers and decorators. Infatuated with the wild and romantic themes of Richard Wagner's operas, poor Ludwig let his imagination and his designers have full rein, and in doing so provided more ammunition for those who thought him mad and were determined to certify that fact.

"He never lived to see his castle completed," the guide informed us. "In 1886, three days after he had been declared unfit to rule, he was drowned along with his doctor."

Poor Ludwig's fate apart, I thoroughly enjoyed Bavaria, as I hope you may. I walked a lot, although I did not kit myself out in the knickerbockers and long, woollen socks which are favoured by the more serious walkers. What I did do was make use of the local tourist offices to provide maps and leaflets and suggestions, and found them, without exception, to be extremely efficient. But efficiency is a characteristic of Germany and you will find it wherever you go, especially if you use public transport. Train and bus timetables dovetail to make the going easier, and that is the kind of efficiency a traveller wants.

A subsequent visit took me along the romantic Rhine, where I encountered other aspects of the German character – in historic Heidelberg, for example, and in razzy Rudesheim, which looks for all the world as if it had been put up by a Hollywood designer specifically for the tourist trade. That visit turned out to be a very jolly cruise, far jollier than I had anticipated, for I had fallen into that trap of believing that Germans have – how shall I put it – a rather ponderous sense of humour. Far from it.

Germany, for me, is a "take us as you find us" country. I've liked what I've found, and hope your experiences there are as pleasant.

John Carter

Germany is one of the most diverse and beautiful countries in Europe. The land stretches from the Alps to the Baltic Sea and encompasses some truly spectacular scenery; the Bavarian Mountains, the Black Forest and the North German Plain have so much to offer that they hardly seem to be true. But Germany is not just a matter of beautiful scenery and exciting cities. There is also the famous German cuisine. There are delicate Rhine salmon, that may be as good as a Scottish fish, and some truly amazing pâtés. Nonetheless Germany is still best known for its heavy food.

The great beer and sausage festivals are one of the greatest expressions of the German spirit. In vast halls and tents hundreds of Germans sing and swing while drinking beer from enormous steins and munching their way through delicious sausages. During these festivals the Germans really let their hair down, and with good reason. Not only is German beer famed far and wide, but the sausages are many and varied. The *Frankfurter Wurst*, named for its city of origin is, of course, the best known of them all. The gift that Germans have for serving everything with dumplings is shown at its best in Westphalia. There they bake the famous *Blutwurst*, or blood sausage, in dough.

Regionality is still the key to Germany, and the German character. The occasional Bavarian will declare that "north of the Danube is abroad, north of the Main is hostile territory". Though this attitude is no longer as pronounced as it once was, it is the legacy of Germany's history. Throughout the story of the German peoples there have been two diametrically opposed impulses, one towards unity and one towards regional independence. Both of these have their roots in the same event. In AD 800 the Empire of Charlemagne stretched from the Ebro to the Elbe and was the most powerful military and cultural force in Europe. In its wake it had brought Christianity and culture to the heathen lands of Europe and had stopped the Moors from crossing the Pyrenees. This great empire had been won by Charlemagne and his knights by sheer force of arms and was held together by the personality of the Emperor himself. When Charlemagne died he left the Empire to his son, Louis the Pious, but it was not destined to survive another generation.

Louis' sons, Charles the Bald and Louis the German, viewed the Empire as private property to divide as they saw fit. Consequently, in 843, the Empire was divided into East and West between the two brothers.

Louis the German became King of all the Germans and laid the foundations for the Holy Roman Empire that was formed in 962, when Pope John XII raised King Otto of the Saxons to the title of Emperor. The Empire founded by Otto was to endure for almost a thousand years and bring a form of unity to Central Europe. The Empire grew with the years until it stretched from the Scheldt to beyond the Oder, embracing within its boundaries all the German peoples. The court of the Emperor was the most magnificent in Europe and the power of the Holy Roman Empire was beyond doubt. It promised to be the expression of German nationalism, but at the same time contained a fatal weakness.

The precedent of gavelkind set by Louis the German when he divided his father's Empire was followed by many of his subjects. Originally the Emperor had to deal with ten Duchies, but the number of important subjects rose as each duke, lord and knight split his estates between his sons, granting to each the rights and privileges that he himself enjoyed. Over the years the powers of the individual rulers increased as they pursued rivalries and, through their powers as electors, alternated the position of Emperor among various dynasties. As the emperors tried to put down rebellions they had to cede even more powers to the individual lords.

Eventually, the dukes and lords within the *Reich* became independent rulers in all but name. They could build castles, maintain armies and levy customs duties within their territories without reference to the Emperor. Not only did peace and unity suffer as wars and feuds proliferated, but trade suffered as well. The right of princes to impose customs duties meant that every few miles a merchant had to pay money to move his goods. The inhibition that this placed on trade, and therefore on prosperity, was enormous. The route that suffered most was also the richest and most important: the Rhine. Castles sprang up along this major trade route, almost within sight of each other, and each demanded a toll on the barges.

The result was that, by 1648, the original ten Duchies had multiplied into some 1,800 lordships. Each duke, baron and elector worked for his own advantage, quite often to the detriment of the Empire. Even without the rivalries and dissension within the *Reich* the task of co-ordinating 1,800 independent rulers was obviously beyond any one man.

It thus came as no surprise to anybody when the Empire fell before the might of Napoleon in 1806. In the turmoil of the French Revolutionary Wars the vast majority of the independent principalities disappeared. The divisive impulse in Germany gained the upper hand as electors and dukes became completely independent kings and grand-dukes.

After the wars, Germany was brought together in the German Confederation. This organisation covered much of the land of the old Empire, but contained only thirty-nine states. Though there were fewer states than in the previous arrangement, there was just as much division, as the kings and grand-dukes jealously guarded their newly-won rights and territories. True unity of action and purpose did not come until 1871, with the advent of the Second *Reich* under Prussian leadership.

The present-day states which make up the Federal Republic of Germany are roughly based on the boundaries that emerged after 1871. Each still exercises important powers within its frontiers and has its own parliament and head of government. However, the Federal Government has a tight control over the states and the country now operates as a cohesive whole.

Perhaps the most beautiful, certainly the largest, of the states is Bavaria. The State of Bavaria now covers much the same area as did the Kingdom in 1806, stretching from Austria to East Germany and from Czechoslovakia almost to Frankfurt. Bavaria had been a duchy long before Louis the German took it for his own; indeed it had been a duchy for two centuries before Charlemagne added it to his empire. In 1180, the Holy Roman Emperor gave the duchy to Count Otto of Wittelsbach, whose family ruled the area until the devastating military defeat of 1918. Throughout the Middle Ages, unlike many other families, the Wittelsbachs managed to keep their inheritance entire. Bavaria thus managed to retain its identity and culture which had always distinguished it from the rest of Germany. At this time, however, the duchy only covered the southwestern area of the present state, the northern and eastern sections being divided into a multiplicity of individual entities. It was as a result of the Napoleonic Wars that the Duke became a king and extended his sovereignty over the much larger area that Bavaria now covers.

It is the area south of the Danube that epitomises the popular view of Bavaria. It is amongst the foothills of the Alps that the great, fairy-tale castles rise into the sky and the leather-breeched mountain men are seen. The town of Garmisch-Partenkirchen, set in the Alps of Upper Bavaria, is the largest winter resort in Germany. It offers reliable snows and a wide range of accommodation. Among the mountains are found many delightful villages, complete with their traditional Bavarian architecture. Onion domes and steep streets dominate the countryside, together with castle-topped hills. Throughout the whole of Upper and Lower Bavaria a certain feeling pervades the air, creating an atmosphere unique to the region.

The capital of Bavaria is the great city of Munich. This large industrial centre has managed to keep its peculiarly Bavarian character despite the fact that it is full of 'foreigners' from elsewhere in Germany and has undergone extensive rebuilding programmes. It has been said that a visitor would learn much more about Munich if he avoided all the sightseeing and spent his time in a beer hall consuming some of the city's most famous products. But apart from steins of *Stimmung* or *Gemütlichkeit*, Munich has many treasures to interest the visitor. This historic city has numerous reminders of its medieval past. Several of the original city gates survive as do many churches and the magnificent Rathaus, which was rebuilt after suffering bomb damage. Facing the Hofgarten stands the Residenz, the rebuilt residential palace of the Wittelsbachs which dates back to the 16th century. Housed within the palace is the magnificent treasury of the Royal House of Bavaria, making the building as much a museum as a palace. Perhaps the most delicate treasure in the Residenz is a small statue of Saint George slaying the dragon, which was completed in the Renaissance style of 1580. Despite its size this statue is encrusted with some two thousand diamonds, four hundred rubies and two hundred pearls.

Though the Wittelsbach dynasty ruled Bavaria for nearly eight centuries and left its mark on the capital, it is the work of the nineteenth-century kings that has come to mean so much to Bavaria. King Ludwig I was a dedicated builder, diverting much of his state and personal income towards the projects he had planned. He was determined to make true his boast that "no one will be able to claim to know Germany without having seen Munich". On his orders Ludwigstrasse was built as a carefully planned whole and many monuments and museums were erected. The city of Munich became the showpiece of Bavaria as the magnificent streets and buildings grew and spread. The efforts of Ludwig I made Munich one of the cultural centres of Europe. His patronage of the arts was magnificent, attracting the best talent in Germany. Ludwig I was an ardent admirer of Ancient Greek architecture and based many of his buildings on Hellenic models. The greatest expression of this style is to be found, not in Munich but some sixty miles to the north, near Regensburg. Standing high above the Danube is the Walhalla built in memory of famous Germans. It is a magnificent copy of the Parthenon in Athens as it appeared when first built.

The building mania of Ludwig I was passed on to his son, Maximilian II and his grandson, Ludwig II. The new Ludwig, who became king in 1864, at the early age of eighteen, was far more interested in German styles of architecture than his grandfather had been. The early years of his reign were unfortunate ones for Ludwig. In 1866 he sided with Austria during her crushing defeat at the hands of Prussia. Five years later he reluctantly took his Kingdom into the Second *Reich*. After these disappointments the King withdrew more and more from public life in search of solitude and peace. Ludwig's first attempt at an escapist retreat was the Linderhof Palace in the Graswang Valley. This palace was based on a hunting lodge of Maximilian II. At first the lodge was merely enlarged, but later it was demolished and by 1878 the palace was completed. The result was a grand, two-storied Rococo building set in beautiful gardens. This magnificent creation was the work of Carl von Effner and took many years to complete. The style of the building and gardens reveal Ludwig's admiration of the Bourbon dynasty of France, with its absolutism and magnificence.

King Ludwig's next architectural extravaganza was influenced by his obsession with Wagner and Teutonic legends. Ludwig was a lifelong admirer of Wagner's operas and this led him into the world of pagan gods and heroes. In 1868, the king decided to build a medieval castle decorated with scenes from Wagner's operas, in a medieval and mythical fantasy. The result was the famous Neuschwanstein Castle.

Built on the site of the medieval castle of Hohenschwangau, this fairy-tale castle soars into the air amid the Bavarian mountains. It took years to build, mainly because of financial difficulties, and was not completed until after Ludwig's death. The interior is a riot of ornate medieval and Byzantine decor, suited to the demands of its royal builder. The majesty of the setting for this dream castle is truly breathtaking, standing as it does on a rocky crag overlooking a lake and forested slopes.

Not content with these spectacular achievements, Ludwig began building an even more magnificent palace on an island: the palace of Herrenchiemsee. Designed to rival "Versailles in all its glory", this palace was never finished. In 1886, King Ludwig was declared an incurable lunatic and taken to Starnberger See where he drowned himself. It is sad to think that the builder of such wonderful castles should come to such an end. But his creations remain as a living testimony to a glorious period in the history of Bavaria.

The historical Duchy of Bavaria forms only a small part of the present state; beyond the Danube lies the territory of Franconia. Upper Franconia, which lies along the Czechoslovakian border, is a land of atmosphere and mystery. The tall mountains and still, dark forests surround the castles and halls where lords and ladies held their courts. It was to these courts that the minnesingers were summoned by the knights and barons to compose and read their rhymes. Here, too, the mastersingers sang in the walled towns to the joy of the citizens. Together, the minnesingers and mastersingers laid the foundations of later German lyric poetry, and inspired Wagner to some of his greatest operas.

In the far north of the region, near the border with East Germany, is a small area where Upper Franconia can be seen at its best. The town of Coburg stands in the Itz Valley, in the hills above the Main, and contains many fine Renaissance buildings. Perhaps the best of these is the Gymnasium Casimirianum, which was built in 1605, though the Rathaus is also a magnificent building. The town is best known for its ruling family, that of Saxe-Coburg-Gotha, whose members married royalty across Europe. Prince Albert, the husband of Queen Victoria, was from this family and a statue of him stands before the Rathaus. Above the town rises an imposing hill which is crowned by a massive castle. The Veste, as it is known, has three lines of defence and is one of the largest castles in Germany. The slopes from the town to the Veste have been turned into a park, which make the setting of the nine-hundred-year-old castle nothing short of idyllic.

North-east of Coburg is the border town of Neustadt. Every day, at noon, a recorded goat bleat sounds out from the Rathaus; a custom which dates back to the days when the town was under siege. The attacking army was trying to starve the town into submission, and had very nearly succeeded, when a tailor had an idea. He decided to sew himself up in a goatskin and frolic around on the town walls making goat-like noises. This display convinced the attackers that the town had plenty of food and so the siege was lifted. That, at least, is the story.

In the mountains lies the cultural centre of Bayreuth. The city had a chequered history, with its castle passing from family to family, until it became part of Bavaria in 1810. Today, it is most famous for its annual Wagner Festival, which attracts opera lovers from far and wide. Wagner had already introduced his revolutionary style of opera when he met King Ludwig II of Bavaria in 1864. This meeting with the builder of Neuschwanstein was crucial to Wagner, who had once been exiled from Germany and was always short of money. The eighteen-year-old king gave Wagner a house and finances and arranged for the staging of some of his operas.

Being financially secure, Wagner was now able to concentrate on completing his masterpiece, *The Ring*. By the time the tetralogy was completed Wagner had been working on it for over twenty years. It had been agreed that the work would first be performed in Munich, in return for the help given by King Ludwig, but Wagner broke the agreement. He decided that his new style of opera needed a new style of theatre, so he built one. Since 1869 Wagner had lived in the mountain town of Bayreuth and he felt that this setting, amid the Teutonic forests, was the proper place for the new theatre. After a series of fund-raising concerts, work began on the wonderful new *Festspielhaus* and in mid-August, 1876, *The Ring* had its triumphant debut. The composer lived in this mountain town until his death in 1883. After his death the annual opera festivals were continued by his widow and sons and they remain a family concern to this day. These landmarks of Europe's cultural calendar are still of great financial importance to an otherwise sleepy mountain town.

Lower Franconia is quite different from the wooded mountains of Upper Franconia. Rolling, oak-covered hills sweep down into river valleys where some of the best German wine is produced. It is often said that a culture manifests itself in its food and drink. By that criterion Nuremberg and Wurzburg are a thousand miles from the beer-drinking centres of Munich and Augsburg.

Wine in Germany is based upon two great grapes: the Riesling and the Sylvaner, though the new Müller-Thurgau is gaining ground. These grapes produce white wine of a quality that is normally good and, at times, extraordinary. The most remarkable thing about German wines, and an important factor in their production, is the fact that they are grown so far north. Nowhere else, except perhaps in Lincolnshire, in England, are vineyards planted so far from the equator. As a result, the wine-growers of Germany are obsessed with the weather. Some of the more dedicated producers will state on their labels at what time of year the grapes were picked and will keep summer wines separate from autumn wines. In France, wines are graded according to the vineyard from which they came and the quality of wine that this vineyard generally produces. The Germans, on the other hand, may name the place of origin on the bottle, but the quality is controlled by the amount of sugar in the must; the must being the juice of the grapes before fermentation.

In 1971 the German Parliament passed new laws which laid down strict guidelines for the grading of wines. *Qualitätswein mit Prädikat* is the top grade, having a must weight of 73 or over. These wines should be made from particular strains of grape and should have no sugar added. *Qualitätswein* must pass tests similar to, though not so strict as, those passed by the *Prädikat* wines. Both these grades are allowed to carry the name of their vineyard on the label. *Tafelwein* covers everything else produced in the country and is not allowed to show a vineyard name.

Franconian wine is unusual among German wines in that it is usually sold in a *bocksbeutel* – a curiously shaped bottle rather like an old flagon – and with oval-shaped labels. These superficial differences signify a different type of wine. Franconia produces wines that are much drier than most and are nearer to the white Burgundy than to the Mosel. In the past, Franconian wines were famed for their ability to last, and in the 1960s a bottle of wine from the famous 1540 vintage was opened. It was quite nice, according to the taster.

The great city of Lower Franconia is the beautiful medieval town of Nuremberg. This city began in 1030 as an Imperial castle which was built by Henry III on a reddish sandstone knoll, where it can still be seen dominating the city. Henry was eager to protect two important trade routes, one from Scandanavia to the Alps and the other from France to Eastern Europe, which crossed on the River Pegnitz at the foot of the Jura. In time the castle attracted artisans to a small settlement under its protection, and the city was chartered in 1219. The growing city soon became a centre of craftsmanship and commerce, achieving independence as a Free Imperial City by the close of the thirteenth century. This status was lost on the fall of the Holy Roman Empire and Nuremberg became part of Bavaria.

The medieval flavour of the city survives to this day in the steeply-gabled roofs and narrow, winding streets of the old town. The central area of the city is still bounded by its city wall, which dates back to 1452 and still has about sixty of its original towers. One of the picturesque houses, with its dormer windows, was the home of Albrecht Dürer, possibly Nuremberg's most famous son. The great artist lived in the building from 1509 to 1528, during which time he produced some of his greatest work. The house itself could be taken to be typical of the architecture of Lower Franconia. The lower stories are built of stone for solidity, while the upper stories are half-timbered, giving a curious, mixed appearance. Set high in the roof are the distinguishing features of the style; the dormer windows. The size and sloped roofs of the windows give the view of Franconian cities an outline that can never be mistaken. The city is a thriving manufacturing and commercial centre, dealing in goods as far ranging as motor cars and toys. A population total of half a million places it amongst the leading centres in Germany today.

Northwest of Bavaria lies the state of Hessen. This area stretches from the Rhine to Kassel and includes the important city of Frankfurt. The state was put together from the earlier states of Hesse-Kassel, Hesse-Darmstadt and Nassau, which themselves were made up of earlier and smaller states. Hessen lacks the historical continuity of Bavaria, but at the same time is more united. There is no cultural break between areas within the state, as there is between old Bavaria and Franconia. The state is an area of wooded hills and spa towns where life can move at a gentler pace; it is only in the great city of Frankfurt that any haste can be detected.

The conurbation is the first thing that greets the visitor when he crosses the border from Bavaria. Frankfurt has never been a great tourist attraction, and probably never will be, but it has long been the financial heart of Germany. Situated near to many important trade routes, not the least of which is the Rhine, the site was long ago recognised as one of great importance. Charlemagne set up his court here more than a thousand years ago, when it was known as Franconofurt.

When Louis the German set himself up as lord of all Germany he decided that he was owed the privileges and properties of the Holy Roman Emperors. One of these was the Pfalz, or Imperial castle, at Franconofurt. Not content with taking over his grandfather's palace, Louis set about improving the site. In 852, he began work on the Church of the Saviour. In the thirteenth century this church was rededicated to Saint Bartholomew and became a cathedral. It was here that the Holy Roman Emperors were crowned after their election, which took place in the city for nearly a thousand years. In the fifteenth century a magnificent, red sandstone tower was added to the cathedral. Standing some three hundred feet above the city, this famous landmark managed to survive the intensive bombing of the Second World War. Today it remains as a lonely reminder of medieval Frankfurt in a largely concrete city.

On the western edge of the urban sprawl lies the town of Höchst. This industrial town was missed by Allied bombers during the Second World War and so preserves much of the medieval charm that was Frankfurt. Timbered houses line the narrow streets that huddle behind the town walls, but it is the Justiniuskirche which is the treasure of the town. This church dates back to the days before Louis the German came to Frankfurt, and has been enlarged and embellished over the years.

The main reason for the existence of Frankfurt has always been trade. In 1240, an annual Summer Fair was started and, in 1330, this was joined by a Spring Fair. Both these events have survived the turmoil of the centuries and are still held. However, their importance has now been overtaken by that of the financial and international business conducted in the city. Frankfurt is now the fiscal heart of the nation, being home to many major banks as well as the Frankfurt Exchange. It is the area around the Turm, the old execution place, that has now become the business centre. Massive office blocks, such as the steel and glass Zurich-Haus, rise into the sky as symbols of the new Frankfurt. The city is not just concerned with the world of high finance, however. It is a major industrial centre, where highly mechanised firms pour out chemicals, leather goods, foodstuffs and books. The city's association with books goes back to the year 1454, when Johann Gutenberg set up shop. Gutenberg was the inventor of moveable type printing, the process that brought books to the mass market. Today, the Frankfurt Book Fair is the main international market for publishers.

To the southwest of Frankfurt is an untypical area of Hessen; the Rhinegau, where some of the best wines in Germany are produced. Here the Rhine, which has been running steadily northwards, runs up against the Taunus Mountains and turns westwards. This means that the right bank faces south, and the slopes are covered in vines. The south-facing slopes make for sunny and moderate weather while the river induces the rising mist that causes 'noble rot'. It is this condition that concentrates the flavour and sweetness of the grape, making possible the much sought after *Trockenbeerenauslese* type of wine. Along this twenty-mile stretch of river are produced many excellent wines, among them the Schloss Johannisberg, Schloss Vollrads and Raunthal. Most of these wines are best drunk on their own, without food, for any extra taste may destroy their delicate flavour.

The rest of Hessen stretches away to the northeast of Frankfurt in a seemingly endless panorama of wooded hills. It was in these dark and mysterious forests that the brothers Grimm wandered in search of tales and legends. After the defeat of Napoleon they were librarians to the Elector of Hesse-Kassel, which enabled them to pursue their chosen line of research. In dark, draughty woodmen's huts the brothers talked to men and women, young and old, assiduously noting down their stories and rhymes. The magnificent collection of folktales and songs that they published was an immediate success and has been translated into over fifty languages. In the atmospheric Teutonic woods of Hessen it is easy to imagine Hansel and Gretel lost and all alone. Indeed, all the Grimms' tales have the air of brooding menace that is to be found in the woods where they had their origins. But it was not only the tales of the Hessen woods that brought fame to the Grimms. Their methods of research laid the foundations for the study of folklore and have been followed by many people since.

In a great crescent, from the Rhine to the Weser, straggles a line of spa towns that are well known across Europe. Perhaps the most beautiful, and certainly the most important of these is Wiesbaden. The city stands in a beautiful setting between the Rhine and the Taunus hills and is now the capital of Hessen. For years the royalty of Europe flocked to the city for the waters, and the social life that went with them. The magnificent palace of the Dukes of Nassau stands along the banks of the Rhine. It is from the river that the best view of its Baroque facade can be obtained. The Dukes' town palace in Schlossplatz is now used as the parliament building for the state assembly.

Tucked away among the wooded hills north of Wiesbaden is the charming valley of the Lahn. Along the length of this valley, from Marburg to Limburg, tiny medieval towns cluster around the castles that afforded them protection in the days when constantly feuding lords roamed the land with their private armies. One of the most impressive of these fortresses is that at Braunfels. The castle here stands high above the river on a mountain top, its turrets and towers striving ever upward into the sky. In Limburg itself there is the mighty, thirteenth-century cathedral of Saint George. This church, unusual in the fact that it has seven spires, is so well blended into its surroundings that it seems to grow out of the living rock. Giessen and Marburg, further upstream, are both ancient university towns surrounded by wooded hills.

After so much scenic beauty amongst the hills and forests of

Hessen, the industrial town of Kassel appears as a rude intrusion. The town is given over to heavy industry, particularly the manufacture of railway equipment, and is the prosperous centre of the area. The Fulda, on which Kassel stands, winds its way northwards into the state of Lower Saxony. It was at the University of Göttingen, which stands on the Leine – another tributary of the Weser – that Otto von Bismarck read law. This great statesman was later to slice through the Gordian Knot of Schleswig-Holstein with the military might of Prussia. The state of Lower Saxony contains two of the three independently governed cities still left in Germany: Hamburg and Bremen. The third is West Berlin, buried in the heart of East Germany.

The importance of the port of Bremen dates back to the Middle Ages, when it was a member of the Hanseatic League. The League was a confederation of free cities which joined together to improve trade and shipping. In 1947 the port of Bremerhaven, at the mouth of the Weser, joined the state of Bremen. This brought the area of the state up to 156 square miles, which made it the smallest state in West Germany. Standing on the Weser, the port handles a vast amount of cargo and is the second most important in Germany. The city has been declared a free port and this has helped industry to expand and develop.

Hamburg is, of course, the most important port in the nation. Thousands of ships sail up the Elbe every year to discharge their cargoes and load new ones. Its history as a port dates back over a thousand years. In 834 the town became an archbishopric, with the aim of converting the heathens of northern Europe. The heathens, however, did not like the idea and in 845 burned the city to the ground. In the next three hundred years, the city was burnt another eight times.

But the economic development of the town as a port continued undeterred. In 1189, the Emperor granted the city special trading privileges and the right to use the Elbe for shipping. Over the years the city steadily extended its powers, privileges and territory along the lower courses of the river. During the Medieval period the city joined the powerful Hanseatic League, a union of free ports which banded together to protect trade and shipping. This legacy of prosperity founded on trade has endured to the present day. Hamburg is still the most important port in Germany. It handles about a third of all the nation's imports and exports, together with half of the transit trade. In all some 45 million tons of goods flow through the port each year, carried by almost twenty thousand ships. It is not only as a seaport, however, that Hamburg has gained fame. Its airport of Hamburg-Fuhlsbüttel is over seventy years old and handles three million passengers each year. Hamburg is truly the port of Germany.

North of Hamburg is the state of Schleswig-Holstein, which was the cause of a short, but bloody, war between the two great states of Prussia and Austria in 1866. The history of

Germany as a whole is one of divided inheritances, disputed territories and rapidly changing ownership, making for a complicated and bewildering story. The past of Schleswig-Holstein, however, is so intricate and bizarre that very few historians even pretend to understand it. The problem in the 1860s, for example, was so involved that it was beyond the comprehension of most of the statesmen who were trying to solve it. Holstein was part of the German Confederation, even though it was ruled by the King of Denmark but claimed by another prince, and Schleswig was not, despite the fact that most of the people living there were German. The division dated back to the time when Louis the German included the county of Holstein, but not the Duchy of Schleswig, into his Duchy of Saxony. Schleswig, but not Holstein, remained a fief of Denmark for seven hundred years from the twelfth century onwards, though not without dispute. Holstein, meanwhile, achieved the status of a Duchy within the Holy Roman Empire. When the Holstein Ducal line died out, in the fifteenth century, the lands were claimed by Duke Christian of Oldenburg, who was a son of a daughter of the House of Holstein. Christian was, by this time, the King of Denmark as well and so brought the Duchies together at last. Holstein remained within the Holy Roman Empire and both Duchies remained outside Denmark, they just happened to have the same ruler. After the Napoleonic Wars, Holstein, but not Schleswig, became part of the German Confederation, the successor of the Holy Roman Empire, but was still ruled from Denmark, as was Schleswig. By the mid-nineteenth century the question "who should own Schleswig-Holstein?" was almost beyond answering. Prussia thought that she should own the Duchies, because they were German not Danish, and she was the dominant power in north Germany, though only Holstein was inside the German Confederation. Austria, as President of the Confederation, thought that she should decide the Duchies' fate, also ignoring the fact that Schleswig was not in the Confederation, and wanted them to be independent of control from both Prussia and Denmark. To cap it all somebody entirely different claimed that he, not the Danish King, was the true Duke of Holstein and backed his claim up with some highly complicated genealogical tables. Finally, the Danes decided to settle the problem by annexing the Duchies, but only succeeded in getting soundly beaten by the armies of Prussia and Austria. The victors then fell out and went to war, with the result that the Duchies became part of Prussia. Today, they form a separate state within the Federal Republic, but a section of Schleswig is now in Denmark again.

History apart, Schleswig-Holstein is fascinating. The western part of the state is a place where the marshy landscape is unbroken by trees and where grazing is about the only activity. Off the coast lie the bleak, windswept North Frisian Islands. The islands are favourite resorts for the Germans, and the most famous is surely Sylt. On Sylt lies the town of Westerland which, with its casino, sports and beaches, is the largest in the islands. Further out to sea stands

Heligoland, an island of increasing importance as a health and holiday resort.

The central part of the state is an area of high land with poor, bleak soils. But beyond this, on the east coast, are rich, fertile wheat fields, interspersed with broad, blue lakes. Vast amounts of grain are produced on the plains of the east coast, but agriculture still only accounts for a tiny fraction of the state's wealth. Industry provides nine-tenths of exports from the area.

The town of Kiel, on the Baltic, is the largest of the industrial cities of Schleswig-Holstein, containing about one in ten of the state's population. It is, of course, the Baltic outlet of the Kiel Canal which runs from the North Sea and is a great aid to navigation. Each year some 80,000 ships pass through this waterway to avoid the tortuous channels around Denmark. For many years the city was the main naval base of Germany, and this heritage is evident in the shipbuilding and heavy industry that still form such an important part of the city's economy. Lübeck, on the Trave River, was once the most important city in the Hanseatic League. As such it has a remarkable collection of fine historic buildings. The Rathaus is perhaps the finest of these and is built in the brickwork so important in the area.

South of Hamburg sprawl the great plains of Lower Saxony, which stretch from Holland to the East German border. The state was put together after the Second World War as an amalgam of Hanover, Braunschweig, Oldenburg and Schaumburg-Lippe; but it is by no means an artificial unit. The people of the area may have been politically divided in the past, but they have always been culturally tied together. Most important of all they speak a common language – Low German. This variant of German dates back to the days of Charlemagne and was the original basis for High, or Standard, German. Low German, as it exists today, preserves many of the hard consonants which have been softened in High German. For instance Low German *Dorp*, meaning village, has become *Dorf* in High German. The language is still widely spoken in the street and many local publications are printed in the dialect, despite the spread of High German. After the War the population leapt by nearly two million, due to an influx of refugees from the east, but this did not alter the basic character of the area.

Crisscrossing the flat land is a system of canals, taking cargoes from the Ruhr to Bremen and Hanover, and from Hanover to Hamburg. The land itself is mainly given over to agriculture and forestry, giving the state a lush scenery unmatched by any other. Equally, it does not have many large urban areas. Apart from Bremen and Hamburg, which are strictly speaking not in Lower Saxony itself, only Hanover tops the half million population mark.

The centre of the rural west is the town of Oldenburg. Though today Oldenburg is just a city in Lower Saxony it was the centre of a state until 1946. Before that date it was the seat of the Dukes of Oldenburg, whose line reached back to the twelfth century. Perhaps the most famous of these Dukes was Christian, who lived in the fifteenth century. He was born the son of Count Dietrich the Happy and Hedvig of Holstein and, in time, succeeded his father. In 1448 he was elected King of Denmark and Norway, leaving Oldenburg to his younger brother, Gerhard. When the line of the Dukes of Holstein died out, Christian claimed the Duchy through his mother and had the might to back the claim up. He was, therefore, responsible for initiating the hideous complexities of the Schleswig-Holstein question.

Gerhard's descendants made Oldenburg into a prosperous Duchy by shrewd diplomatic manoeuvring. During the Thirty Years' War the Duke gained the right to charge a toll on ships passing up the Weser to Bremen, which gave an important financial boost to the state's finances. Eventually the direct line of Oldenburg died out and the Duchy came into the hands of the Tsar of Russia in 1773. However, he soon gave it to Frederick Augustus, who was not only his cousin but also held the Bishopric of Lübeck. Lübeck bordered Holstein. Frederick, as Duke of Oldenburg, now had a tenuous claim to Holstein. The Duchy of Oldenburg, Holstein apart, willingly joined the *Reich* in 1871.

One of the city's most important treasures dates back to its days as an independent Duchy. The great ducal palace of 1615 was built in the Renaissance style and is still an imposing building. It now houses an impressive museum of art and culture. But perhaps the most mysterious feature of Oldenburg is not to be found in the city itself. To the south lies the Ahlhorn Heath and on the heath lies the Visbecker Bridegroom. This is a 360-foot-long pile of enormous granite blocks and has stood on the windswept heath since the dawn of history, an enigmatic legacy from the past.

It is Hanover that is the political and industrial heart of Lower Saxony. The city is, perhaps, most famous as the centre of the former Kingdom of Hanover. The state had its origins in the marriage of George Louis, heir to Brunswick-Calenberg-Göttingen, to Sophia Dorothea, heiress to Brunswick-Lüneberg. It is not surprising that the official name of the new Electorate was rarely used. The state was known as Hanover, after its principal city.

In 1714 the Elector of Hanover became the King of England and Scotland as George I. For well over a century the two countries were ruled by the same sovereign, though by separate administrations, and each influenced the policy of the other. During the French Revolutionary Wars the Electorate was lost to Britain. With the return of peace the old Electorate was reorganised as a kingdom and was greatly increased in size. The two countries separated in 1837 on the accession of Queen Victoria, for Hanoverian Law forbade a woman from wearing the crown. Ernest Augustus became the King of Hanover, but his son lost the kingdom to Prussian aggression as an indirect result of the thorny Schleswig-Holstein Question. Until the end of the Second World War Hanover was a part of Prussia, but its territory now makes up about four-fifths of the state of Lower Saxony.

The modern city has been built on the ruins of the old, which was heavily bombed in the war. Not only have new streets, factories and houses sprung up, but old buildings have been restored to their former grandeur. One of these is the magnificent Rathaus, which took fifteenth-century masons nearly fifty years to build. Other buildings have not been restored, among them Saint Aegidien's Church, the shattered outline of which stands as a memorial to the war victims.

As the former capital of a kingdom and the present capital of a state, Hanover has been well endowed with public buildings. The Leine Palace, built in the 1630s, has been extended over the years. As the neo-Classical residence of the Hanoverian Court, it was rebuilt after the Napoleonic Wars to house the increased regal splendour of the King and his government. More recently, it has been extended by a dynamic, modern structure to give more room and office space. This was necessary because the building now houses the Parliament of Lower Saxony, with all its attendant services and bureaux.

Each spring Hanover hosts an important international trade fair at its Fair Grounds in the southeastern suburbs. These grounds are among the most impressive sights in Hanover. There are twenty-two halls, three enormous fair buildings and an open-air exhibition ground whose size is truly staggering. The fair reflects the city's importance as a manufacturing centre and the industrial hub of the state of Lower Saxony.

Over the hills, in the upper Weser Valley, stands the town of Hamelyn. Though this is a lovely old market town, built around the Abbey of Saint Boniface, Hamelyn is best known for an event that probably never happened. Many theories have been put forward to explain the legend of the Pied Piper, who first led away all the rats and then all the children of the city. It is now generally accepted that the story is an amalgam of two historical events, preserved in a rather jumbled form in folk memory. The first was the visitation of the Black Death which struck the town in the fourteenth century. The plague was carried by the fleas of the large black rat, which was new to Europe. Thus the appearance of hundreds of rats became associated with evil times. The exodus of the children has two possible origins. First, the days of eastward expansion, when young men poured out of the established towns to seek their fortunes. The second, and more convincing, theory is that it refers to the Children's Crusade of 1212. In this tragic event twenty thousand German children set out to free the Holy Land by their love and innocence. They crossed the mountains behind Hamelyn into Italy and never returned, many being sold into slavery. Quite how the piper in multi-coloured garb fits into all this still baffles folklorists.

Further southwest, across the border into Westphalia, stretch the depths of the dark Teutoburg Forest. Today the woods, which lie on the slopes of an arm of the Hartz Mountains, are crossed by many roads and enfold the towns of Bielefeld and Detmold. But two thousand years ago they formed a dark and forbidding territory. In AD 9 three Roman legions crossed the Rhine in their glittering armour, with flowing banners, to put down the Germanic tribes. More than a tenth of the entire Roman professional army was sent in under the command of Publius Varus. They met the Germans, led by a chief named Arminius, in the Teutoburg Forest and were never heard of again. Many years later another Roman army crossed the Rhine and reached the Teutoburg Forest. Spread amongst the trees and over the boulders they found thousands of bleached and moss-covered skeletons. The armour no longer glittered and the banners had long since rotted, but the soldiers of Varus had been found. Today, an enormous monument to Arminius, or Hermann, stands on a mountain in the midst of the forest.

If Lower Saxony was a collection of states with a common culture and identity, the same cannot be said of Westphalia. Officially known as Nordrhein-Westfalen, this state was put together after the war from two areas with quite different traditions. The line between the Rhineland and Westphalia dates back more than a thousand years to the boundary between the Saxons and the Franks. Language differences that have their roots in that period are still very much in evidence in the streets of Warendorf and Goch. A more recent division that strikes just as deep is that between Protestant and Catholic. Throughout the state the division is about equal, but the population of individual localities may be almost entirely of one persuasion or the other.

A quarter of the state's area is given over to forest and, in all, two-thirds of its land is used for some form of agriculture. Despite this, the combined agricultural wealth accounts for barely a thirtieth of the annual product. The reason for this is simple: the state includes the mighty Ruhr.

For many years the industrial heartland of the Ruhr has been the 'Forge of Germany', producing vast quantities of iron and steel. Extending under the area is one of the largest coal deposits in the world. It produces most of Germany's coal and has been the basis of the remarkable prosperity of the region. Five of the towns in the region have populations in excess of 350,000: Essen, Gelsenkirchen, Duisburg, Dortmund and Bochum. The population density for the area is around 9,000 people per square mile, one of the highest in the world.

By the time of Louis the German, coal mining had begun in the Ruhr and it has continued ever since. But it was not until the early part of the nineteenth century that the industrial potential of the area was fully realised. Since that time the story of the Ruhr has been inextricably bound up with the story of the Krupp family.

In 1587, Arndt Krupp arrived in Essen, which was then an independent state under the control of a convent and an abbey, and it was here he decided to settle. No sooner had he done so than plague broke out in the city. In the confusion that resulted, Arndt Krupp was able to buy vast tracts of land from citizens who were only too eager to flee the city. When the panic was over and land prices rose again, Arndt Krupp found that he was a very rich man. For several generations the Krupp family extended their wealth and power until they became the virtual rulers of the town of Essen.

In 1811, Friedrich Krupp founded the family's steelworks, but it was his son, Alfred, who made it an international success. Alfred was an undoubted eccentric, but he was also a genius. He believed that the smell of manure helped him to think, so he had his study built over the stables and constructed ducts to carry the smell upwards. The plan must have worked because he came up with the cast-steel cannon with which he armed Prussia. It has been said that without Krupp's guns Bismarck would not have had the military muscle to solve the Schleswig-Holstein Question by force. Without the guns, Bismarck would have had to find the real answer to the Question, a feat that would probably have proved too great even for him.

The Krupps, meanwhile, steadily acquired wealth and prestige. After the Franco-Prussian War of 1870-71 Krupp guns became the mark of a strong army and the weapons were sold to over forty nations. By the time Friedrich Krupp took over the firm in 1887 the family was immensely rich. Friedrich was to more than triple this already mighty fortune.

Fritz, as he was known, was a cunning businessman. With the full might of the Krupps' research team behind him he was able to manipulate the world's arms market by using the 'defensive and offensive weapons seesaw'. First he offered nickel-steel armour that was impervious to standard artillery shells. Naturally enough, the world's major governments bought the armour. Then Krupp announced that he had developed chrome-steel shells that could smash the nickel-steel armour, and armies and navies fell over themselves to buy these. It was not long before the great Krupp's foundries began manufacturing high-carbon steel that could protect ships against chrome-steel shells. Again nations were forced to buy or their fleets became obsolete. Inevitably, Fritz Krupp then came up with a shell that could smash the new armour.

In 1902 this remarkable man committed suicide after a major scandal and left the entire works and fortune to his daughter. It was, however, considered unthinkable that the great German arms industry should be in the hands of a woman. The Emperor himself set out to find a suitable husband for Bertha Krupp and found him in the shape of Gustav von Bohlen und Halbach. This stiff Prussian aristocrat, who changed his name to Gustav Krupp von Bohlen und Halbach, did sterling service for the Second *Reich* during the First World War and played a major part in rearming Germany in the Twenties and Thirties. By the opening of the Second World War the personal fortune of the Krupp family was almost beyond belief. They owned over eighty industrial works, over a hundred other firms and over forty foreign works as well as sizeable holdings in nearly two hundred other corporations. During the War Gustav relinquished control of the vast industrial empire to his son, Alfried. At the Nuremburg War Trials Alfried was convicted and had all his possessions, including the Krupp works, confiscated. But the industry could not do without Krupp and, just after the Korean War broke out, the Krupp fortune was restored. Even so, the Krupp Empire was doomed. Arndt Krupp, only son of Alfried, announced that he did not wish to take over the family business and relinquished his inheritance for an income of half a million pounds a year. In 1967, Alfried died and Krupp's became a public corporation. The hold that the family had exercised over Essen for almost four hundred years was over.

South of the rich industrial state of Nordrhein-Westfalen is the rather poorer Palatinate, known as the *Pfalz* in German. The only natural mineral resource of the state is the pumice of Neuwied which is quarried extensively. The population density of the state is around 500 per square mile, far below that of the whole country and insignificant when compared to the Ruhr. The only towns to achieve any size are those along the Rhine Valley: Koblenz, Mainz and Ludwigshafen.

It is in this state that the Rhine appears at its best, just as it does on all the tourism pamphlets. Here the Lorelei sang her beautiful song of death to any that would listen, luring hapless sailors onto her rock; a rock that can still be seen today. The gleaming river winds its tortuous route between towering hills, each seemingly capped by a castle. These castles are reminders of the days when the Rhine was a rich, but not very safe, place. Ships, full of precious cargoes, plied the waters of the main trade route of Germany. The rich ships attracted bandits and the land would have been a lawless place had it not been for the castles. Many were built to protect the ships and the villages, and they did a splendid job. But many of the fortresses were built to extort cash from the merchants. Under the guise of 'customs tolls' a very lucrative protection racket was run by the knights of the Rhine, though they often had to suffer the consequences. The vast majority of castles along the river have been destroyed at least once, and some several times. But that does not matter today. The castles make a romantic backdrop to the splendid scenery of the Rhine and are places of interest for the visitor.

The Palatinate may be short on natural resources for industry, but it is rich in another commodity. It produces the best of the Mosel wines. The Mosel Valley runs southwest from Koblenz to Trier. The city of Trier is often claimed to be the oldest in Germany and this may well be true. When Caesar conquered the town in 58 BC it was already well established. Indeed, its roots may date back to 400 BC.

The wines of the region also have an ancient history. Many hundreds of years ago the Prince-Bishop of Trier lay at death's door, and none of his physicians could help him. It was then that one of the Bishop's tenants arrived with some wine from Bernkastel. The Bishop tried a sip and felt a bit better. After demolishing two whole bottles, the Bishop declared himself cured and named the wine as the best doctor in the land. To this day the *Bernkasteler doktor* is one the best, and most expensive, wines of the Mosel. Further upstream are grown the great wines of Piesport and its surrounding villages. At their best, these wines are gentle and delicate, but with more flavour than is found in wines from the French Moselle.

Squeezed between the Palatinate and the French border is the important state of the Saarland. This region has been fought over by French and German rulers for centuries, swapping hands with incredible frequency. It only became wholly part of Germany in 1957 and still has economic links with France.

The most important industries of the state are coal mining and iron and steel production, which employ by far the largest section of the workforce. Most of the industry is centred on the city of Saarbrücken, the state capital. This city of over 100,000 inhabitants dates back to pre-Roman settlements, but gets its name from Sarrabrucca, a royal castle above the Saar river. The city is also the cultural centre of the state, where opera, ballet and symphony concerts are performed regularly. There are some remarkable examples of Baroque architecture within the city, including the Elector's Palace and the Ludwigskirche, designed by Stengel.

The modern state of Baden-Württemberg covers a large area of southwest Germany and is bounded by the Palatinate, France, Switzerland and Bavaria. The state includes some of the finest scenery in Germany and some of the loveliest cities.

Heidelberg stands on the River Neckar just upstream of its junction with the Rhine. This city is famous for many things: its castle, its university, its streets and its barrel. The great Heidelberg Tun was built in 1663 and can hold the equivalent of a quarter of a million bottles of wine. It is so large that a stairway had to be built so that visitors could reach the top. But this enormous size did not daunt the dwarf, Perkeo, who is claimed to have drained the tun of wine. The setting of the old city is so romantic as to almost defy belief. The houses and churches cluster between the river and the rock that towers above them, topped by the castle ruins. In 1693, a disastrous fire swept through the city and destroyed it. Undaunted, the citizens set to work rebuilding their town and produced a masterpiece. Round every street corner a fresh view of spectacular German architecture greets the visitor, all dominated by the castle. The castle was built over a period of some seven hundred years but was destroyed in the

seventeenth-century War of Orleans. Today, it stands as a noble ruin overlooking the city.

Further up the Neckar Valley, amid the Swabian Mountains, stands the capital of the state, Stuttgart. This city is a major transport and industrial centre for the whole state. It has been the capital of Württemburg since 1482, throughout the transition from County, through Duchy and Kingdom, to State. It was here that Daimler-Benz set up their factory, a firm that is still important to the city. The heavy industry of machine manufacture is another industry of prime importance to the city, as are the textile, precision engineering and wood and leather goods trades. The city is also a large clearing centre for the region's wine and fruit.

The city's appearance belies its industrial character. Only about a quarter of the city's land is built on, the rest being divided between farmland, parks and forest. It is, perhaps, only in Stuttgart that suburban housing estates are interrupted by centuries-old farmhouses surrounded by grazing cattle and hanging vines. The forests that cover about a quarter of the city's area are not only an important source of timber, but also a playground for its inhabitants.

Southeast of Stuttgart, on the Bavarian border, stands the town of Ulm. The city is famous in history both for the decisive battle in 1805, when Napoleon smashed an Austrian army, and for the 'flying tailor of Ulm'. In 1811, this enterprising individual decided to entertain the visiting King of Württemburg by flying across the Danube on a pair of home-made wings. Watched by the royal visitor and a crowd of thousands, the daring tailor jumped from the city walls and fell straight into the river.

On the right bank of the Rhine, above Karlsruhe, stands the immensity of the Black Forest. This is a great misnomer, for it is neither black nor a true forest. It gained its name from the masses of dark green conifers that spread across the area, but they have hardly any undergrowth and so should not be called a forest. The scenery of the area is truly astounding and is a great draw for the thousands of tourists who flock to the area. Some, however, come for the gentler charms of Baden-Baden. This romantic spa town still caters for the civilised, as it has done for centuries. The hot springs are an important attraction, visitors paying large sums to lie in sticky mud or drink unusual-tasting liquids. On the other hand many come to Baden-Baden for the casino.

It can be seen that Germany is a land of infinite variety and beauty. A place where wine and beer are produced at their best, and the people know how to enjoy them. With its industrial power and potential, Germany is obviously a nation with a great future, while its great historical legacy is a reminder of its long and romantic past. Germany is truly a beautiful land.

Hamburg, the most important port in Germany: (previous page) the Rathaus; (top left) tugs on the River Elbe; (top right) the Rathaus and the Alsterfleet; (left) small sailing boats moored in the Aussen-Alster; (above) a ship steaming down the Elbe, north of Hamburg docks, and (facing page) houses on the east bank of the Elbe at Wedel, one of Hamburg's attractive suburbs.

Hamburg: (left) the pleasant atmosphere of Die Wein Stiege; (above) swans on the Alster Fleet, with the Binnen Alster beyond the bridge. Facing page: (top left) the Reeperbahn area; (top right) a shady path beside the Binnen Alster; (bottom left) the view from the Alsterpavillon Cafe and (bottom right) the elegant interior of the shopping precinct opposite the Alsterpavillon on Jungfernstieg.

21

Hamburg: (top left) the Atlantic Hotel overlooking the Aussen-Alster; (top right) tugs moored beside the north bank of the Elbe; (left) the Neustadt from the south bank of the Elbe; (above) the blue waters of the Binnen Alster and (facing page) the startlingly-modern TV Tower which dominates much of the skyline of the city.

Flensburg (this page) is a picturesque naval base in Schleswig. It was first chartered in 1284 and has maintained its importance as a Baltic port on the Flensburg Fjord ever since, despite being captured and pillaged several times during the intervening centuries. Facing page: the main shopping precinct in Kiel. Though the great canal linking the North Sea with the Baltic is, perhaps, Kiel's most famous sight, it is not the most interesting. The city is a major fishing port and the fish market is one of the most colourful in Germany, while Kiel Week is one of Europe's great regattas.

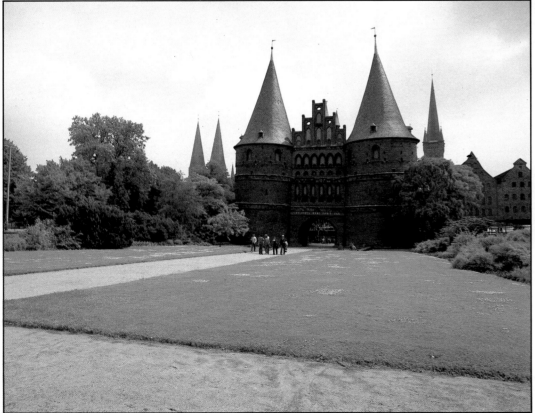

Lübeck (this page) is the largest port on the Baltic coast of Germany. It was chartered as a Free City in 1226 and soon became a leading city in the powerful Hanseatic League, which dominated trade in northern Europe during the middle ages. With the disintegration of the League in 1630, Lübeck lost much of its importance, but prosperity came again following the construction of the Elbe-Lübeck Canal in 1900. The Rathaus (above and top left) is a fine example of the brickwork for which the city is famous, particularly the black-glazed bricks of the curious, turretted upper storey. Left: the massive towers of the Holstein Gate, which was built in 1477. Facing page: the 12th-century cathedral at Ratzburg on an island in the Ratzburger Lake.

Lüneburg (this page) escaped World War II remarkably lightly and still retains many of its old buildings, making it one of the most interesting cities in Lower Saxony. Top left and top right: the 13th to 15th-century Rathaus and the lively market. Left: the flea market. Above: riverside houses. Facing page: a view typical of the landscapes south of Uelzen.

Situated deep inside East Germany, Berlin, once the capital of a united Germany, still finds itself under the control of the four occupying powers, but is now divided by the Berlin Wall into eastern and western sectors. Far left: the stark Soviet War Memorial which was built with stones from the Reich Chancellory, East Berlin. Left: the Neptune Fountain, Alexander Platz, East Berlin. Below: the Bismarck Memorial in the Tiergarten, West Berlin. Facing page: (top left) the Berlin Wall and Potsdamer Platz from the west; (top right and bottom left) the Brandenburg Gate seen from West Berlin and (bottom right) the famous Checkpoint Charlie on Friedrichstrasse.

West Berlin: (top left) the Bellevue Palace in the Tiergarten, the official Berlin residence of the President of the Federal Republic; (left) the Charlottenburg Palace, which contains a variety of museum galleries and exhibits. Above and facing page: the dramatic Kaiser Wilhelm Memorial Church. Originally a Romanesque church built in the 1890s, it was left in ruins by the war and though it was never rebuilt a strikingly-modern tower was added in the 1960s.

The Charlottenburg Palace (these pages) was begun in 1695 and completed just four years later. It was named after Sophie Charlotte, queen of King Frederick I of Prussia, and eventually gave its name to the entire surrounding area. Though originally a palace, the building now houses an extensive museum with exhibit-filled rooms such as: the Red Braid Room (left); the Reception Room (above left); the Porcelain Room (above) and the Golden Gallery (right). Overleaf: (left) the Cafe Kranzler and (right) the Kaiser Wilhelm Church, both on the Kurfürstendamm.

West Berlin: (top left) the Potsdamer Yacht Club on the Wannsee; (top right) the Kaiser Wilhelm Church; (above and facing page) the Glienicker Bridge, which crosses from the American sector of West Berlin into East Berlin at Klein-Glienicke, and (right) the Spandau Citadel of 1560-94, one of the finest Renaissance fortresses in northern Germany.

Berlin: The Charlottenburg Palace (above) lies opposite the Greek and Egyptian museums (top left), the later housing the famous bust of Nefertiti; (top right) the 500-foot-tall Funkturm, which was built in 1926 for the German Broadcasting Exhibition and now houses a museum; (left) the Victory Column and (facing page) the interior of the modern section of the Kaiser Wilhelm Church.

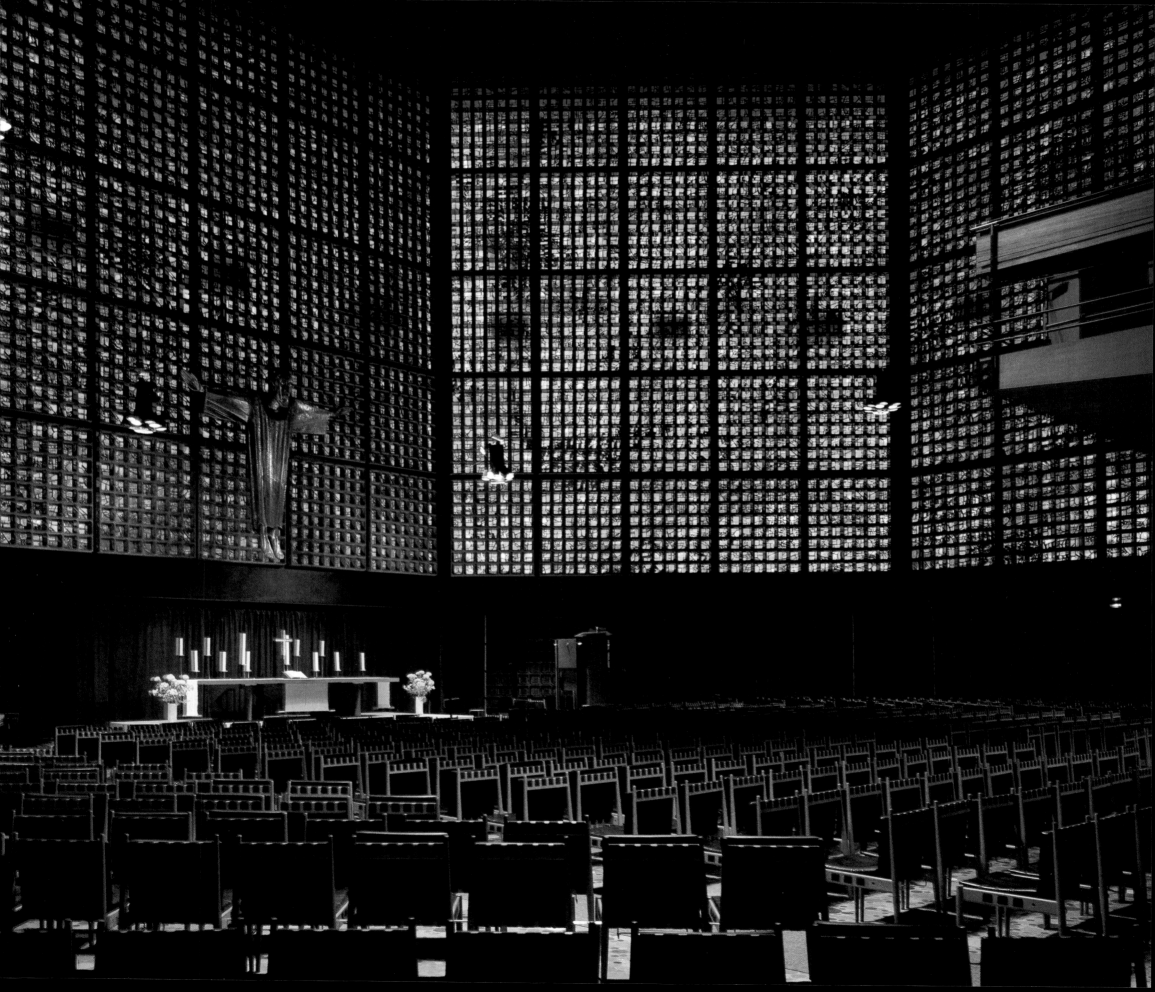

Hanover (this page), the capital of Lower Saxony, is one of the largest industrial cities in Germany and one of the most attractive. Above and top right: the railway station. Facing page: the River Weser near Hamelin.

The town of Hamelin (these pages) has a long and distinguished history which dates back to at least AD 800, when a small village stood on this site. Over the centuries the town became a member of the Hanseatic League and a focus for the warfare which spread across Germany during the 17th and 18th centuries. During the Second World War the town escaped almost unscathed and remains one of the most historically important in the area. The best-known story of the town, however, concerns the Pied Piper, who is reputed to have led away first the rats and then the children of the town. Each year citizens of Hamelin re-enact the drama (this page). Facing page: (top left, top right and bottom right) the Market Square and (bottom left) Allemarkstrasse.

Münden (these pages), near the confluence of the Werra and the Fulda, is one of the most picturesque towns in Lower Saxony. Top left: the Rathaus. Top right and facing page: the old town with its characteristic church spire. Above: the red-tiled roofs of the town. Right: one of several pedestrianised streets in the town.

Top left: the Baroque Rathaus at Münden. Top right: the mansard-roofed Schloss Besichitizung, near Kunz. Above: yachts and an autobahn bridge near Fulda. Right: a rural house between Göttingen and Münden. Facing page: the Main at Frankfurt, from the Flosser Bridge.

The fact that Heidelberg (these pages and overleaf) was almost entirely destroyed by the French in 1693 means that the majority of the important buildings in the city date from the 18th century and include some magnificent Baroque architecture. Facing page: a panoramic view of the city. Top left: the Market Square, with the famous pink castle on the hill beyond. It is in the cellar of this ruined castle that the Heidelburg Tun, a barrel able to hold 49,000 gallons, can be found. Left: a fountain in the Market Square. Above: the Bridge Gate seen across the Old Bridge, both erected in 1786. Overleaf: (left) the Old Bridge and (right) a general view of the city and the Neckar River.

Top left: the Water Tower, one of the main landmarks of Mannheim. Top right and above: the Old Bridge in Heidelberg, which carries a statue of Athena as well as one of the bridge's patron Saint Johannes Nepomuk. Right and facing page: the Neckar at Hirschorn. The town was founded in 773 and is one of the oldest in the valley.

Top left: a small fountain in an evening street scene in Michelstadt, Hesse. Top right: Klingenberg and the River Main. Left: Meselbrunn Castle, which stands in the heart of the Spessart Mountains. Above: the black-and-white timbered buildings of Freudenberg contrast with a modern concrete structure hidden amongst the trees. Facing page: Miltenberg, which stands perched on a hillside above the River Main in Bavaria.

Due to the fact that Bamberg was once divided into the Bishop's Town and the Burghers' Town by the Regnitz River, the old Town Hall (left) stands in the middle of the river. Top left: Klein Venedig (Little Venice), Bamberg. Top right: the four spires of the 11th-13th century cathedral dominate Bamberg. Above: the 15th-century Old Main Bridge in Würzburg. Facing page: the still waters of the Main at Kitzingen.

Nuremberg has long been renowned as a city of skilful and clever citizens, and has given many inventions to the world, including the clarinet, pocket watch and numerous mechanical toys. It is also known for its medieval beauty, including the Schöner Brunnen fountain and the Frauenkirche (facing page and above) in the Hauptmarkt. Top right: Pottenstein. Right: Kipfenberg Castle at Altmuhltal.

The walled, hilltop city of Rothenburg (these pages) is one of the most picturesque medieval cities in Germany. According to legend it was saved from total destruction in the 1630s when a citizen outdrank the invading forces by emptying a three quart jug of wine at a single draught. Facing page, above and right: the Town Hall and the Market Place. Top left: the double-arched Röder Gate. Top right: Mark's Tower.

Facing page: the picturesque main street in the small town of Langenburg, which stands beside the Jagst River. Right: the balcony bar and spectacular view from the castle at Langenburg. Bottom right: the neatly laid out formal gardens at the castle of Langenburg. Below: a fine Baroque church by the roadside near Ellwangen, Wurttemburg.

As the capital of Bavaria, Munich (these pages) has attracted more than its fair share of fine architecture. Above: the twin onion domes of the Frauenkirche, erected in 1488 and long a landmark of the city. Top right: the Gate of Victory. Right: the New Rathaus. Facing page: the Maximilianeum, built for King Maximilian II a century ago, now houses the Bavarian Parliament and Senate.

To the northwest of Munich proper is Nymphenburg Castle (above, top left and top right), a fine palace which was used as the summer residence of the Electors and Kings of Bavaria. Today it is open to the public and provides an elegant venue for summer concerts. Right: the twin towers of the Frauenkirche. Facing page: the elaborate Olympia Park, where the Olympic Games were held in 1972.

Munich: (top left) the Angel of Peace, which stands beside the Prinzregenten Bridge to the east of the city centre; (right) Karlsplatz, one of Munich's more important squares. Once a year, Munich celebrates Oktoberfest (above, top right and facing page) when the locals and visitors watch processions and crowd into halls intent on enjoying a sample of the city's brews.

Top left: the Hotel Hans, near Entfeldmuhle. Top right: the Rathaus of Memmingen, an important spa town which was once an Imperial Free City. Left: the small town of Mittenwald in its spectacular Alpine setting. Above: the Lech flowing over a wier at Landsberg, where many of the Baroque buildings were designed by Dominikus Zimmermann. Facing page: the attractive Maria Gern Church near Berchtesgaden. Overleaf: (left) Ramsau, near Berchtesgaden, and (right) Berchtesgaden.

Previous pages: (left) the Ettal Monastery, near Oberammergau, and (right) the elaborate Rococo interior of the monastery church at Rotenbuch. Top left: the winter sports resort of Füssen. Left: St Columan Church, near Füssen. Above: Nesselwang. Top right, facing page and overleaf left: Neuschwanstein, the magnificent fairy-tale castle built in the last century for King Ludwig II of Bavaria. Overleaf right: Linderhof Castle, near Oberammergau, also built for King Ludwig II.

Facing page: the magnificent Neueschloss at Meersburg, Baden-Wurttemburg. Top left: the still, misty waters of Lake Constance. Top right: a lakeside building near Meersburg. Left: a church near Urlau. Above: Lake Constance at Lindau.

Left: a landscape of fertile fields near Waldshut, just north of the Swiss border. Bottom left: a water fountain in a square in Löffingen, a small town in the Black Forest east of Freiburg. Bottom centre: a view across the rooftops of Laufenburg. Bottom right: a carved, wooden roadsign at Löffingen. Facing page: the bridge across the Rhine at Laufenburg, which links the German and Swiss banks of the river.

Top left and facing page: hire boats lined up on Titisee, an idyllic lake in the heart of the Black Forest. Top right: vineyards near Staffen. Left: an ornate building at Titisee. Above: a passenger cruiser on Titisee.

Left: orderly vineyards climb a hillside near Freiburg. Bottom left: a road through the Black Forest near Freiburg. Below: a romantically-sited hotel in a secluded valley in the Black Forest. Facing page: a road winds through a valley near Titisee.

Freiburg im Breisgau (these pages), with a population approaching 200,000, is the main city of the Black Forest region. It has long based its prosperity on the wood output of the forest, producing furniture, paper and timber. In recent years the city fathers have insisted that any new building should blend in well with the age-old character of the city. The modern buildings (left) show this policy in their steeply-gabled roofs and tiny dormer windows. When time has mellowed these structures they will harmonise with the old city far better than modern buildings elsewhere. Below and below far left: the Cathedral which, since 1827 has been the seat of a Roman Catholic Archbishopric. It was begun in the early 13th century and, when it was completed by 1500, was the only German cathedral built entirely in the Gothic style. Below left: the Schwaben Tower. Below: Rathausplatz. Facing page: (top left, bottom left and bottom right) the quiet, early-morning scene at the market in the Münsterplatz and (top right) some of the street musicians who liven up a day in town.

When, in 1715, Karl Wilhelm, Margrave of Baden-Durlach, decided to build a new city for himself he chose a site near the Rhine and named it Karlsruhe, which means 'Karl's Rest'. He constructed the entire city on a fan-shaped layout with the two wings of his palace (top right) marking the angle at which the arms of the fan divided. Above: the neo-Classical Protestant Church of 1816, designed by Fr Weinbrenner, in the market place (right). Facing page: a weir on the River Murg at Gernsbach.

The town of Baden-Baden (these pages) retains the elegance of its 19th-century popularity when the wealthy and aristocratic of Germany came to this spa-town in great numbers. Top left: the largest church in the town. Left: the Trinkhalle Promenade. Above: the tranquil Baden-Baden Gardens. Facing page: (top right) the Baden-Baden Gardens; (bottom left) the Trinkhalle and (bottom right) one of several horsedrawn carriages available for hire in the town.

Baden-Baden: (top left) cafe tables and the fine view to be gained from the 14th-century New Castle; (top right) the twin-spired church on Augustraplatz; (left) a collection of flags in the Casino Gardens and (above and facing page) the New Castle.

Capital of Hesse, Wiesbaden has long been a meeting place of international figures and today maintains its position as a leading conference centre: (above) the elaborate ceiling of the Russian Church and (top right) the Hesse State Theatre. Right: the Niederwald Monument, erected in 1877 to celebrate the re-establishment of the German Empire and constructed almost entirely by public subscription. Facing page: the church and Klopp Castle at Bingen.

Facing page: (top left) the Drosselgasse in Rüdesheim, famous for its Rhenish hospitality; (top right) the pressing room of the Kloster Eberbach vineyards, the source of much of the local hospitality; (bottom left) vineyards around the Abbey of St Hildegard, near Rüdesheim and (bottom right) the pilgrimage centre of Bornhofen, with one of its two castles, on the banks of the Rhine. Right and below: the little town of Assmannshausen, famous for its wines. Bottom right: the town of St Goarshausen, which began life as a 13th-century fishing village. The tall, white tower on the riverbank formed part of the 14th-century town walls, while the Katz Castle on the hill behind dominated this section of the Rhine.

As a major trade route of the Middle Ages, the Rhine saw a proliferation of castles such as the island fortress of Pfalzgrafenstein (top right), which served as a customs house. Top left: the Mouse Tower at Bingen, which commemorates the death of Bishop Hatto, who was bitten to death by mice on this island. Left: a passenger boat on the Rhine near Bingen. Above: the wine cellar at Kloster Eberbach. Facing page: the Rhine at Lorch. Overleaf: (left) Reichenstein Castle, once the home of robber knights, was renovated in 1899, and (right) a vine-decked side valley of the Rhine.

The many castles along the Rhine Gorge were built for a variety of reasons, some to protect merchants and others to extort customs dues from them. The imposing fortress of Marksburg (above and top right) was first built in about 1200 and its defences were added to and improved on for the next 500 years, until increasingly effective cannon made it useless as a military installation. Right: the 14th-century Pfalzgrafenstein. Facing page: the 12th-century Burg Stahleck, which was extensively restored earlier this century.

The Lahn Valley contains some of the most romantic places in Hessen: (top left) the solid defences of the castle at Runkel, on the Lahn River; (top right and facing page) the seven-spired Cathedral of St George at Limburg, downstream of Runkel, which was erected in the 13th century; (left) the castle at Diez and (above) the Stiftskirche. Overleaf: (left) the Deutches Eck at Koblenz, where the Mosel meets the Rhine, and (right) the magnificent castle overlooking the Mosel at Cochem.

The Mosel Valley is one of the foremost wine-producing regions of Germany and enfolds some charming towns dedicated to the grape: (top left) Bernkastel and the tower of 14th-century St Michael's Church; (top right) the church at Beilstein; (left) Punderich; (above and facing page) Traben-Trarbach, which is surrounded on three sides by the river. Overleaf: (left) the Mosel at Cochem and (right) a forest landscape near Boppard.

Left: the small town of Lieser on the Mosel. Right: with its sheer walls, turrets and magnificent location Eltz Castle is one of the finest in the valley of the Mosel. Bottom left: one of many cruise boats powering downstream past the charming town of Traben-Trarbach. Below: the castle at Cochem. Facing page: a ruined castle overlooking the lower Mosel.

While the town of Bernkastel has made its name abroad through the wine which it produces, any visitor will be pleasantly surprised by the charm of the place: (above) the road which leads to the Market Square; (right) a narrow, timber-framed house in the Market Square; (far right) the church of St Michael. Top right: the fine fountain and timber-framed houses of Monschau, in the valley of the Rur. Facing page: Monschau.

Though an important link in the defences of the Roman Empire along the Rhine, Bonn (these pages) began its march to greatness only when the Prince Electors of Cologne moved their capital here 700 years ago. During their residence at Bonn, the Prince Electors built a magnificent palace (left and above) which now houses the famous university. Top right: a building near the university. Right: the interior courtyard of Poppelsdorfer Castle, which also dates back to the days of the Electors.

The bustling river port of Cologne derives its name from the fact that it was once a Roman colony, but it is the great medieval cathedral (these pages and overleaf left), with its twin towers, which dominates the scene in the city. The foundations were laid in 1248, but work stopped three centuries later, when the towers were only half finished. It was not until 1842 that work was restarted and the spires were not finished until 1880. Overleaf right: the cathedral at Münster.

Top left: the main square of Bremen, second largest port in Germany. Left: the Renaissance facade of the Bremen Rathaus. Above: an imposing statue representing Freedom in the Market Square of Bremen. Facing page: (top left) the Schloss Senden at Wasserburg; (top right) Burg Vischering, near Wasserburg; (bottom left) a street in Münster and (bottom right) Münster Central University Building. Overleaf: the castle at Cochem.